GET CRAFTY

TOYS AND GAMES

Vivienne Bolton

DP
DEMPSEY
PARR

Editor
Barbara Segall

Art Direction
Full Steam Ahead

Design Team
Design Study

Photography
Patrick Spillane

Photographic Co-ordinator
Liz Spillane

Styling
Bianca Boulton

Project Management
Kate Miles

The publishers would like to thank Inscribe Ltd., Bordon, Hants. for
providing the art materials used in these projects and
Sophie Boulton for her assistance.

First published in 1998 by
Dempsey Parr
Queen Street House, 4-5 Queen Street, Bath
BA1 1HE

24681097531

Produced by Miles Kelly Publishing Ltd
Unit 11, Bardfield Centre, Great Bardfield, Essex CM7 4SL

British Library Cataloguing-in-Publication Data
A catalogue record for this book is available from the British Library.

ISBN 1-84084-400-0

Printed in Italy

Contents

Snake

This beautiful sinuous snake can be made from bottle tops. You will need to collect a lot of bottle tops, so it may be worth asking friends to save them for you. By combining different colored tops you could create a multi-colored snake and if you saved only one color of bottle tops your snake would still be dramatic. The silver shimmers and the closely fitted bottle tops give the appearance of scales when wriggled along the floor. The snake's head is made from a cork and his bright red tongue is a piece of felt, cut to shape and pushed into the cork.

You will need:

Hammer

Large nail

Piece of wood

Bottle tops

Strong string

Scissors

Cork

Glue

Paint & paintbrushes

Small piece of felt

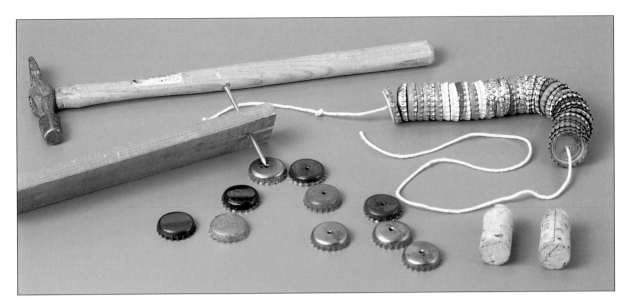

1 Hammer a nail through a piece of wood near its end. You can then hold the wood and position the nail to make the hole in the center of the bottle top.

When all the bottle tops have holes in them thread them onto the string. Think about your color coordination. A snake like this one will need approximately 70 bottle tops.

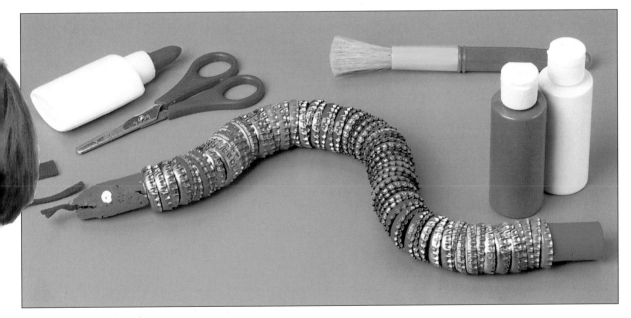

2 Attach a piece of cork to each end of the string of bottle tops. One end will be the tail—paint it green. The other end will be the head—paint this green also and add two spots for the eyes. Cut a small piece of felt into the shape of a snake's tongue and press it into the cork with the point of the nail.

OVEN-BAKE CLAY
Pocket Pets

These cute little pets don't need feeding or cleaning out, just a little loving! The animals are made from oven-bake clay, simply shaped and pressed together. Give the dog big soppy eyes by using a white flattened ball and laying a black eyespot on top of it. Place the black eyespot carefully as that is what gives them character.

The dog collar is another important item. Be sure to give your pets a tag with your telephone number on it in case they wander off! Make a water bowl and bone—and maybe a few doggy toys would be a good idea. The kennels are made from recycled milk or juice cartons. Paint them in bright colors and write your pet's name above the entrance.

You will need:

Oven-bake clay

Modeling tool

Empty milk or juice carton

Scissors

Paint

Paintbrush

Large flat lid for
the cat's basket

1 To make the dog, soften the clay between your fingers then shape the body and feet. Take a small piece of dark brown clay and roll out a thin tail. Make a flattened sausage shape for the ears and lastly make the eyes and collar. Assemble your little pet and bake it in the oven according to the manufacturer's instructions.

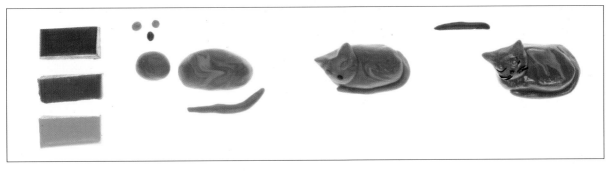

2 To make the cat you will need orange, yellow, and brown clay. Roughly mix equal quantities of orange and yellow clay. Shape the body first and then the head. Use your fingertips to pinch out the ears. Roll out thin pieces of brown clay to make the cat's whiskers and eyes and position them on the face. When you are happy with the shape of your pet, bake it in the oven according to the manufacturer's instructions.

3 To make this roomy kennel you will need an empty milk or juice carton. Cut out the shape and mark the entrance. Paint the kennel in attractive colors. You might want to write your pet's name above the entrance hole.

If you don't have any oven-bake clay make your pets from Plasticine.

PLASTIC CONTAINERS AND OVEN-BAKE CLAY
Bowling

Enjoy a game of bowling whenever you like with these brightly decorated recycled drink containers. You will need six containers to make a set. Paint them in bright colors and decorate them with colored stars. If they get knocked over too easily, pour some sand into each one to make them heavier. Mini- or table-bowling can also be fun. You could make a set to take away on vacation. They are made from oven bake clay. Take turns with a friend to see how many skittles you can knock down with each shot.

You will need:

Empty drink containers

Paint

Paintbrushes

Sand, for weight

To make mini-bowling you will need:

Oven-bake clay

1 Wash out the drink containers well. Leave upside down to drain. Screw the lids on tightly and your skittles are ready for painting. Begin by painting a base coat.

You may need two layers of paint. When the base coat is dry, paint on the decoration. When all your skittles are painted and decorated they are ready for use.

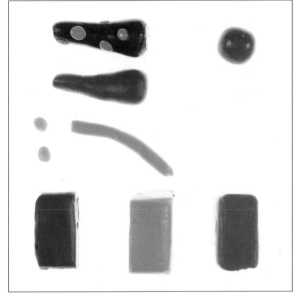

2 To make these mini-bowling pins you will need oven-bake clay in three colors. Divide the clay into equal pieces and shape the skittles. Use oven bake clay of a different color to make flattened ball shapes and press them onto the bowling pins. Shape a ball and when your ball and bowling pins are ready, bake in the oven according to the manufacturer's directions. You might want to decorate a small box in which to store your mini-bowling pins.

A set of mini-bowling pins would make a good Christmas cracker gift or party favor.

A full size set of bowling pins could be used at a school sports day or fund-raising event.

Magic Pictures

This fishy picture changes from black and white to color quite magically. Make one to delight a younger brother or sister. Choose your picture carefully: an empty black and white hillside could turn into a green pasture covered with sheep, or a bare table top could have a birthday cake appear on it.

Use brightly colored felt-tip pens to color your picture. It is a good idea to keep the shapes simple. If you don't have a plastic folder you might be able to recycle a piece of clear plastic from a carton.

You will need:
Thin cardboard or paper

Scissors

Marker and felt-tip pens

Plastic folder

Tape

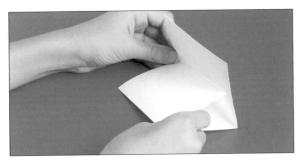

1 Take a sheet of thin cardboard or paper and fold it carefully into three equal sections as shown in the picture.

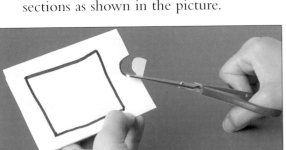

2 On the front flap mark out a rectangle and the finger grip space. Cut away the finger grip space.

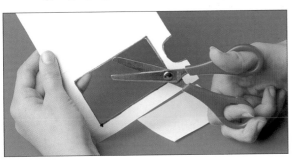

3 Open out the cardboard and cut out the rectangle. This is the front of the card.

4 Draw a decorative border on this front frame. Cut a separate piece of paper the same size as one section of the card and draw on your design, using felt-tip pens.

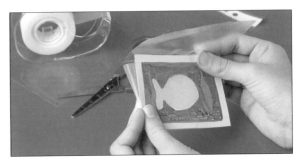

5 Slip your picture into the plastic folder with the top against a fold. Trim the plastic to the picture. Stick the back to the plastic.

6 Use a marker pen to draw an outline of the picture on the plastic. Now take your card and open it out flat.

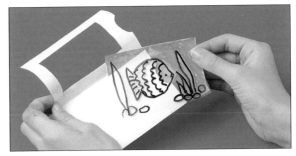

7 Fold the bottom flap into the middle. Slip the plastic-covered picture over the bottom flap. The bottom flap is now between the colored picture and the outlined picture on the plastic flap. Fold the top flap down over the plastic. Grip the plastic and paper and pull; the picture will appear in color as you pull it out.

Games Board

This neat little games board is made from thick cardboard and a piece of narrow craft wood. You will need a little time and patience to paint the squares neatly but it is worthwhile when you consider the entertainment you will get from a home made games board. Here we show how you can make home-made checkers from oven-bake clay. You could use two colors of buttons or pebbles instead. Maybe you have a small set of chess pieces at home that could be used. A personalized board would make a lovely present.

You will need:

A small board-shaped piece of thick cardboard

Paint & paintbrushes

Pencil

Ruler

Scissors

Thin piece of strip wood from a craft shop

Glue

Oven-bake clay

Match box

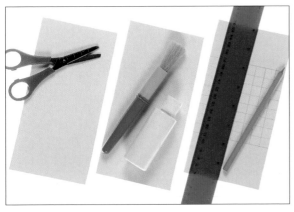

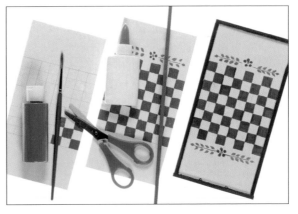

1 Paint the card in a light color. Paint the strip wood in a darker color. Leave to dry in a safe spot. When the paint is dry, carefully mark out the games board with eight rows of eight squares. Use the ruler to measure the squares. Leave space at each end of the board to keep pieces not in use during the game.

2 When you are satisfied with the marked areas, paint in the darker color. When the paint is dry, use the scissors to cut the strip wood and glue into shape to form an edge around the board. Decorate the board with an attractive pattern at each end and touch up any parts of the edging that need painting.

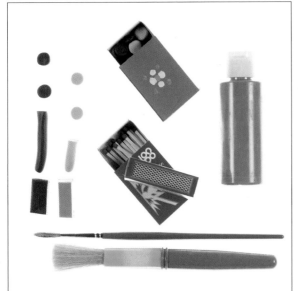

3 Shape the checkers from oven-bake clay. You will need eight counters in each color. It is best to roll out a sausage shape of clay and cut slices to size. Bake them in the oven following the manufacturer's directions. Paint a small matchbox in the darker color and decorate it to match your games board. Use the box to store your checkers.

If you had an old tray you might want to recycle it into a games board. Ask an adult for help; you may need to sand the tray down with sandpaper first as well as decorate it using several coats of paint!

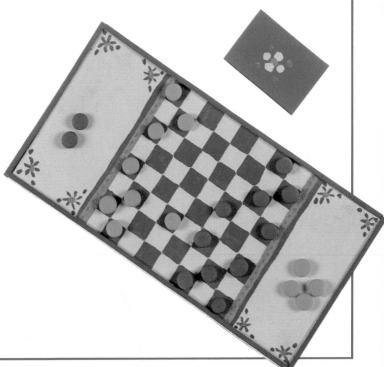

Dollhouse

Make a cute little dollhouse for a miniature doll or bear to live in. This house is made from two boxes. Use any card you may have over to make miniature furniture. You may want to have a look round for some small matchboxes or other containers to recycle as furniture. Colored paper makes good wallpaper, as does wrapping paper. Use a piece of fabric to make carpets and rugs, and don't forget some pictures to go on the walls. Decorate the outside of your house with paint, creating a cheerful summery scene for your doll to live in.

You will need:

Two shoeboxes

Scissors

Tape & glue

Large paper clips

Paint & paintbrushes

Paper & cardboard

Small boxes

Felt-tip pens

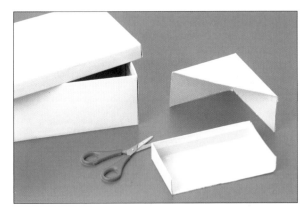

1 Use one of the boxes to make the house. Cut a corner off the other box to make the roof and cut the lid so that it fits inside the house as the upstairs floor.

2 Place the shoe box that will be the house up on one end. Use tape to attach the roof piece you have prepared at an angle to the top of the house. Use glue and tape to stick the floor section into place. Hold the floor in position with the large paperclips while the glue is setting.

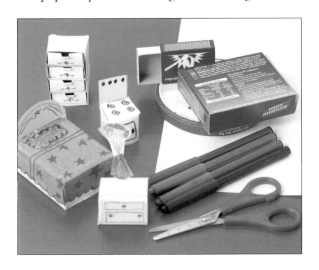

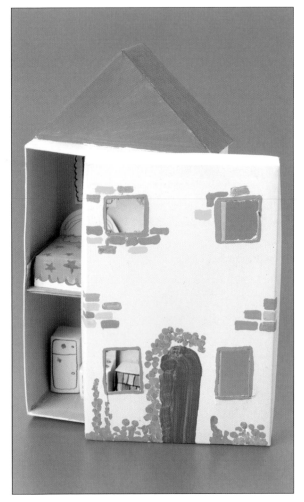

3 When the glue is set your house is ready to decorate. Paint the roof a rich reddy brown and the walls pale pink. Make a front for the house from the other shoe-box lid and cut out windows. Paint a bright front door and flowers and make your house summery and cheerful.

4 Miniature furniture is easy to make from scraps of paper and small boxes. Cover boxes with white paper to make kitchen equipment and colored paper for furniture in other rooms. Use felt-tip pens to outline shapes and decorate the pieces. Don't forget wallpaper and rugs and maybe some pictures on the walls.

SPONGE BOARD
Blow Soccer

occer is a very popular sport. Enjoy a game of blow soccer on a rainy day by making your own table-sized soccer field. This field has been made with a piece of sponge board. If you wanted to make a more long-lasting field, you could get an adult to help prepare a piece of chipboard or plywood. You will also need green felt to cover the board, although paint would give a reasonable surface. The game is played using drinking straws and table tennis balls. Each player begins with an equal number of balls and sees how many he or she can blow into the opposite goal. Once you become more professional, you might want to play a more traditional soccer game with one ball decorated using a marker pen to look like a real football.

You will need:
Sponge board
Green felt
Scissors
Glue
Shaped craft strip wood
Paint
Paintbrushes
Cocktail sticks
Colored paper
A shoebox
Drinking straws
Table tennis balls

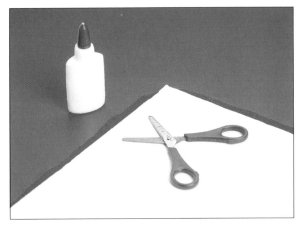

1 Cut out the felt slightly larger than the board. Spread the board with glue and press the felt onto the board.

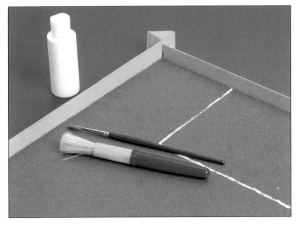

3 Glue the edging in place and use the white paint to mark out the goal mouths and center line.

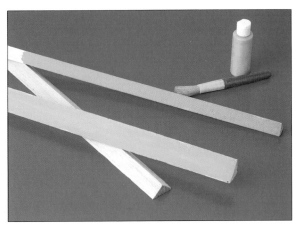

2 Cut the edging to size and paint it yellow. As well as both sides and ends of the pitch, you will need four small pieces to make the corners.

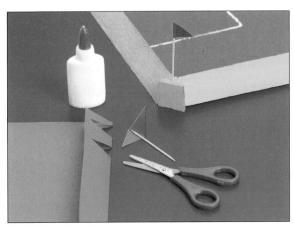

4 Press a cocktail stick into each corner of your field. Fold the colored paper in half and cut out four flag shapes. Glue the flags onto the cocktail sticks.

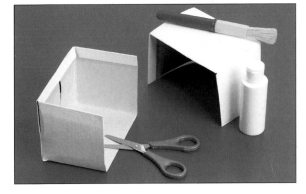

5 Cut the shoebox in half. Paint the halves white and when they are dry place them on the field at opposite goal mouths. Put the table tennis balls in position and it's time to challenge someone to a game!

CARDBOARD
Toy Cars

These cute little cars are great fun to make and given a push will whizz along a smooth surface. The wheels are made from milk or juice container lids, cocktail sticks and straws. The car chassis is cut from either colored cardboard or the sides of a recycled grocery box.

You will need:

Thick cardboard

Scissors

Masking tape

Paint

Paintbrushes

Four juice or milk carton lids

Straws

Cocktail sticks

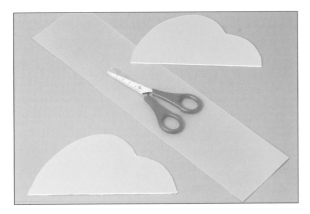

1 Begin by drawing two side views of a car. Cut them out. Next cut out a long rectangular shape. The width of the rectangle decides how wide the car is.

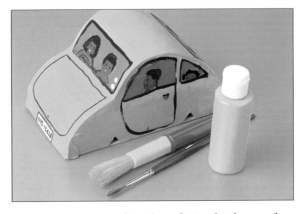

4 Cut a piece of card to fit in the base of the car. Tape it in place. Your car is now ready to paint and decorate. You could paint on a family sitting in the car.

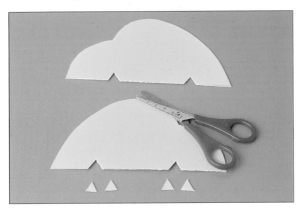

2 Use the scissors to cut out two small v-shapes to form the wheel arches. The wheel axles will run through these v-shapes. The wheel axles will be held in place by the base of the car.

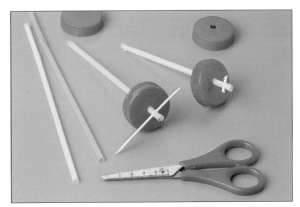

5 To make the wheels each lid will need a hole made through its center. Push the end of a straw through the hole. Now use a cocktail stick to hold it in place. Break the ends off so that the wheel turns.

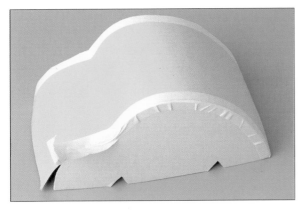

3 Now you are ready to assemble your car. Use masking tape to attach the long rectangular shape to the car sides. Do this and you will see the car take shape.

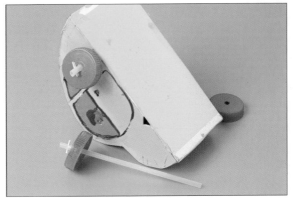

6 Push the wheel axle all the way through and attach the second wheel. Cut off any long pieces of straw to fit the car. Now make and fit the second axle.

Green Lentils and Fabric
Juggling Balls

Juggling is a great skill to develop. It takes time and patience but can be most fulfilling. Make yourself some juggling balls and a set for a friend and practice together. These juggling balls are made from printed cotton fabric and filled with uncooked green lentils. Lentils are a perfect filling as they will give the juggling balls some weight and be easy to grip. They are also quite economically priced—and—if you stop juggling you can cook the lentils for supper!

1 Cut a rectangle of fabric and fold it in half. Sew seams along the side edges. Sew strong stitches close together or ask an adult for help and use a sewing machine.

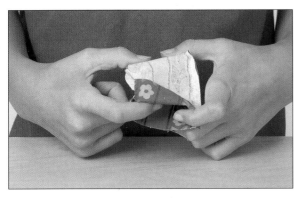

2 Turn the bag shape right side out.

3 Half fill the bags with green lentils.

Juggling balls would make a great birthday gift for a friend.

4 Close the bag making a triangular shape by bringing the two side seam ends together and neatly fold the edges inside to allow for the final seam.

5 Sew the edge together firmly.

You will need:

Fabric

Scissors

Green lentils

Needle and thread

FABRIC AND CARDBOARD
Doll's Bed

You will need a shoebox to make this comfy bed for a doll or teddy bear. The bed is made from the box and the bedhead is made from the lid. The bed will look stylish covered with brightly colored gingham fabric or you could decorate some plain fabric using fabric felt tip pens. Cover the fabric with small flowers or draw out a patchwork spread pattern.

You will need:

A shoebox

Fabric

Scissors

Glue

Lace

Fabric painting pens

Polyester wadding

Needle and thread

1 Turn the box upside down and cover it neatly with fabric. When attaching fabric it is a good idea to put the glue on the box rather than the fabric. Use a length of gathered lace to create a frill.

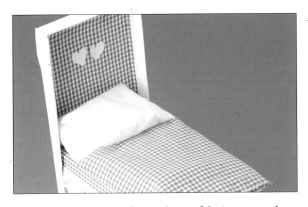

2 Stick a piece of matching fabric onto the inside of the lid of the shoebox to make the bedhead and glue the bedhead onto the base. Cut pieces of polyester wadding to size and sew on fabric covers to make the mattress, pillow and duvet.

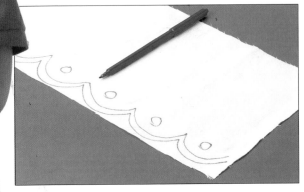

3 The fabric to make this bed is decorated with fabric painting pens. Measure how much fabric you will need to make the frill around the bed. Decorate the frill with a scalloped pattern.

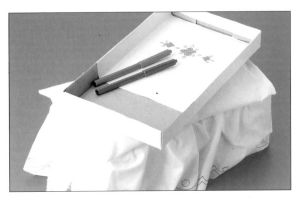

4 Gather the fabric into a frill and glue it onto the bed. Make a mattress from polyester wadding and sew on a fabric cover. Decorate the inside of the box lid to make a matching bedhead.

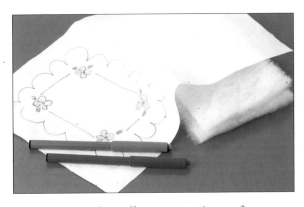

5 To make the pillow cut a piece of polyester wadding to a suitable size, fold a piece of fabric over the pillow shape and cut out the cover. Decorate the pillow cover using fabric pens. Use your needle and thread to sew the pillow up.

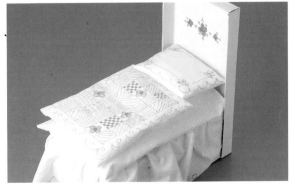

6 Make a duvet from a piece of polyester wadding and fabric. Use fabric pens to decorate the duvet cover so it looks like a patchwork quilt. Copy your scalloped design for the border.

23

CARDBOARD AND CRÊPE PAPER
Party Hats

Making party hats is a great way of getting the party spirit going. These hats are quite easy to make from card and crêpe paper, and can be decorated with glitter and junk jewelry.

Try your hand at making a complete set of party hats for a special family meal or celebration. Make Queen and King crowns for the grown-ups and fancy coronets or colourful jester's hats for all the children.

You will need:
Thin cardboard

Scissors

Needle and thread

Crêpe paper

Glue

Glitter

Hair band for the tiara

1 Cut a length of card that will go around your head with a small overlap.

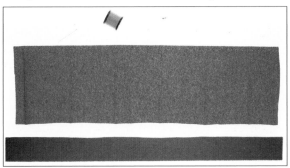

2 Next cut a wide piece of crêpe paper the length of the cardboard. This will need to be quite wide; have a look at the illustration to get an idea of the size. Sew a line of running stitch along one of the long sides of the crêpe paper.

3 Glue the crêpe paper onto the cardboard.

Paint pasta shapes gold or silver and decorate with glitter and use to decorate your crown.

4 Next, glue the paper-covered cardboard into a hat shape. Pull the ends of the thread to gather the crêpe paper and tie a knot. Use crêpe paper to cover a small disk shape of card and glue that over the center of the hat. Decorate the hat with colored paper or card and glitter.

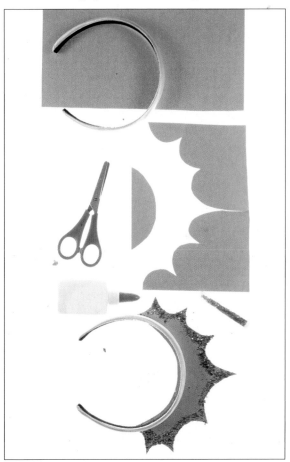

5 This sparkling tiara is made with a hair band and gold card. Lay the hair band onto the card and draw out the shape. Cut out the tiara shape and decorate it with glitter. Attach the tiara to the hair band and leave to dry.

Model Theater

Make a model theater and stage your own pageant this Christmas. You will need a shoebox and colored paper to make the theater. Once you have decided on a storyline you can get a script together and decorate sheets of paper to use as scenery.

Make small model trees and furnishings from card and paper. Cut out actors from thin card and use tape to attach them to sticks. You can have as many actors on the stage as you can handle. So you may need a friend or two to help when staging your big production.

You will need:

Shoebox

Scissors

Colored paper

Felt-tip pens and crayons

Glitter

Tape

Thin cardboard

Sticks (kebab sticks would be the right size or recycle some disposable chopsticks)

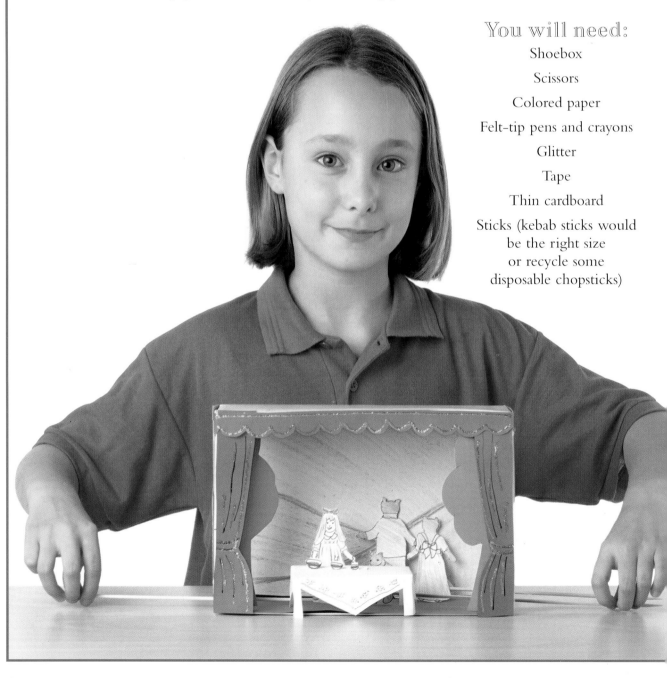

1 You will need a shoebox to make your theatre. Stand it on its side and cut out an opening on each end. Your actors will enter the stage from these openings.

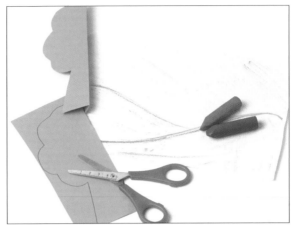

4 Cut a piece of paper to size and decorate it with crayons to make a scene that suits your play. Attach it to the back of the box; this will be your scenery backdrop.

2 Use colored paper to decorate the front of the theater. Make curtains and frills. Use a black felt-tip pen to mark out the gathers. Accentuate the edges with glitter.

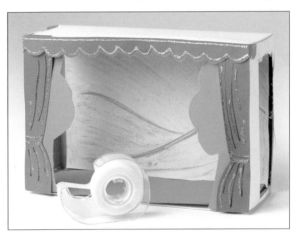

5 Cut out colored paper shapes that match your scenery. Use sticky tape to attach them to the inside edges of the curtains; these are called the wing flats.

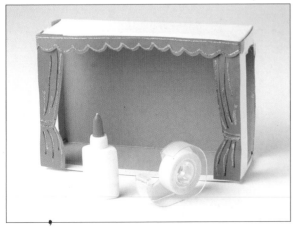

3 Glue the curtains into place using sticky tape for difficult corners.

6 Draw your actors onto thin cardboard cut out from the lid of the shoebox. Color them in using felt-tip pens and cut them out. Use tape to attach them to the sticks. Remember they will have to enter the stage through the side entrances, so check for height.

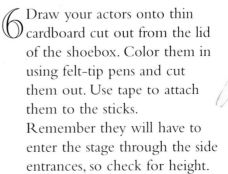

SHOEBOX
Guessing Box

Guessing boxes, filled with interestingly shaped items such as damp squidgy sponges, pine cones or plastic spiders, can be great fun at parties. When players put their hands through the hole their imaginations will turn a damp sponge into something very strange, not the kind of thing one would normally want to touch without looking at it first! Another game to play with a guessing box is to put in a variety of similar things, such as vegetables. Then the players have to guess what they are, by touch.

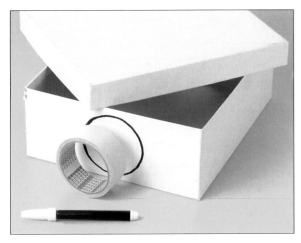

1 Use the circular object to draw a hand-hole on one side of the box.

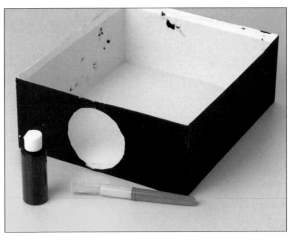

3 Paint the outside of the box and lid black. If necessary, apply two coats.

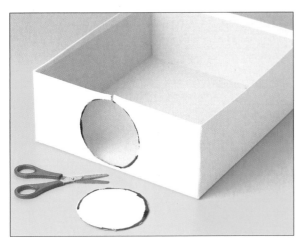

2 Cut out the hand-hole. It is easier to start the hole by cutting down from the top. This cut will be hidden by the lid.

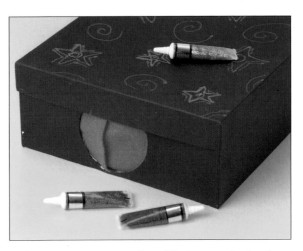

4 Use tape to attach a fabric curtain in the box over the hole and decorate the box with glitter or colored paint.

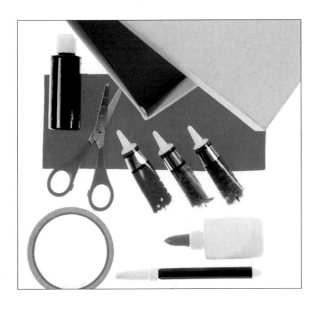

You will need:

Large shoebox

Circular object to draw around

Pen

Scissors

Paint

Paintbrush

Tape

Piece of fabric

Glitter

FABRIC AND WOOL
Cloth Doll

A soft cloth doll is nice to cuddle up to and looks pretty lying on a pillow as decoration. These dolls are made from cotton fabric and are cut out in a "gingerbread man" shape. Their hair is made from wool and they are dressed in simply shaped clothes tied with ribbon. A cloth doll can be made large, as a bed decoration, or tiny, to live in a dollhouse or be a "pocket" doll. Practice painting faces on a piece of paper to get the shapes right before you paint your doll's face on.

You will need:

Fabric in a flesh color for the doll

Felt-tip pen

Scissors

Needle and thread

Polyester stuffing

Paint

Paintbrush

Wool

Ribbon

Patterned fabric for the doll's dress

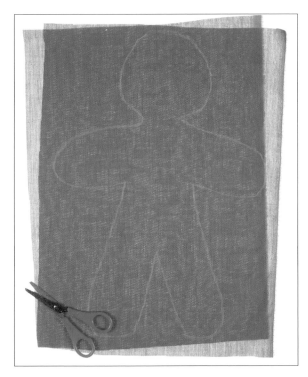

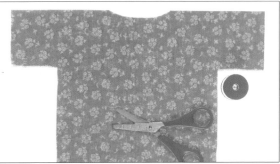

3 Use the cut-out doll as a pattern to cut a simple dress shape and sew the edges.

1 Draw a doll shape onto a double layer of fabric. Remember you will need a neck shape that you can sew around and cut out. Look carefully at the picture to get an idea of the shape you need to draw.

4 Turn the dress the right way out and sew a hem along the bottom of the fabric.

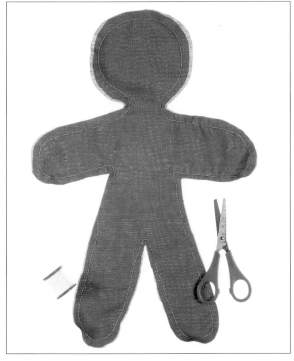

5 Dress your doll and paint on a face. Make hair by winding the wool around a piece of card then sewing a "parting" across the middle. Attach the hair with glue.

2 Sew around the drawn line, remembering to leave a gap to turn the fabric out. Fill it with stuffing, then cut the doll shape out.

6 Tie a ribbon belt in a bow around the waist. Now your doll is ready to enjoy.

Index

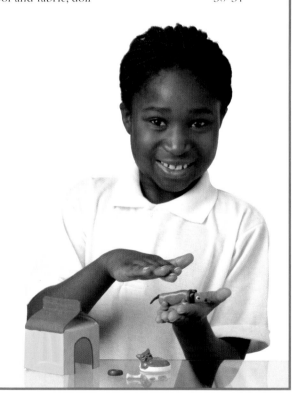